# ROCK
# INSTRUMENTALS

### Arranged by Chad Johnson

ISBN 978-1-4768-2305-8

HAL•LEONARD®
CORPORATION
7777 W. BLUEMOUND RD. P.O. BOX 13819 MILWAUKEE, WI 53213

Visit Hal Leonard Online at
www.halleonard.com

# Beck's Bolero

By Jimmy Page

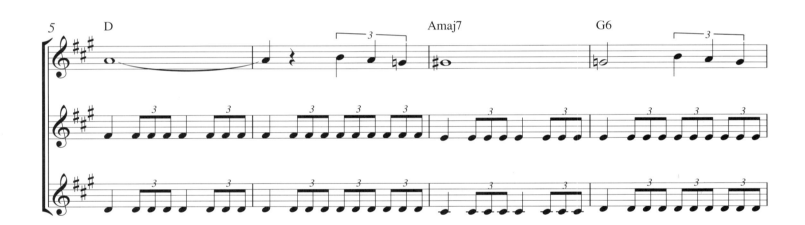

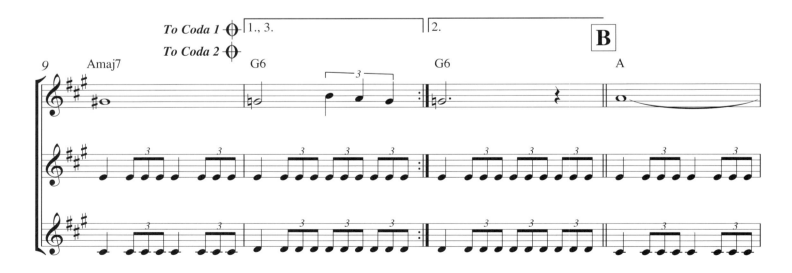

# Cissy Strut

By Arthur Neville, Leo Nocentelli, George Porter and Joseph Modeliste, Jr.

# Europa
## (Earth's Cry Heaven's Smile)

Words and Music by Carlos Santana and Tom Coster

# Frankenstein

By Edgar Winter

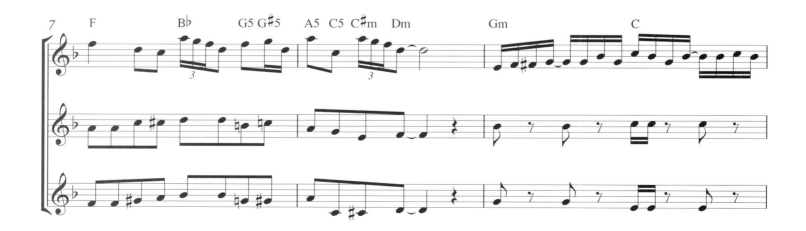

# Jessica

Words and Music by Dickey Betts

# Green Onions

Written by Al Jackson, Jr., Lewis Steinberg, Booker T. Jones and Steve Cropper

# Misirlou

Words by Fred Wise, Milton Leeds, Jose Pina and Sidney Russell
Music by Nicolas Roubanis

# Perfidia

Words and Music by Alberto Dominguez

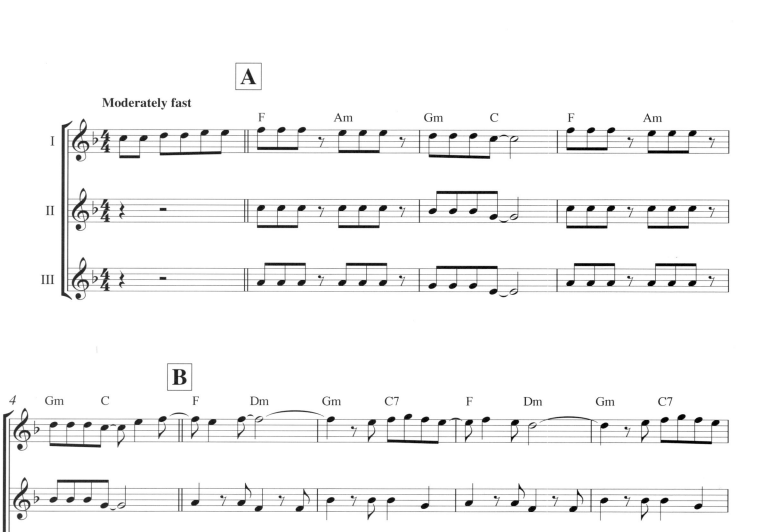

# Pick Up the Pieces

Words and Music by James Hamish Stuart, Alan Gorrie,
Roger Ball, Robbie McIntosh, Owen McIntyre and Malcolm Duncan

# Pipeline

By Bob Spickard and Brian Carman

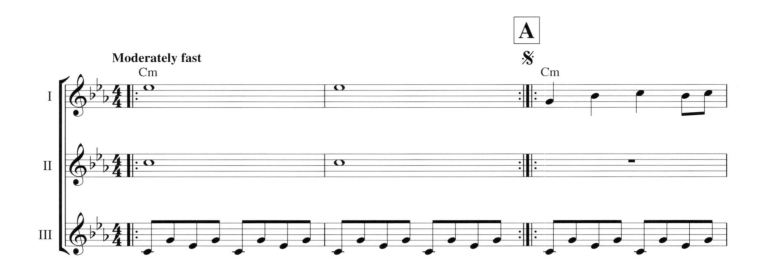

# Rebel 'Rouser

By Duane Eddy and Lee Hazlewood

# Sleepwalk

By Santo Farina, John Farina and Ann Farina

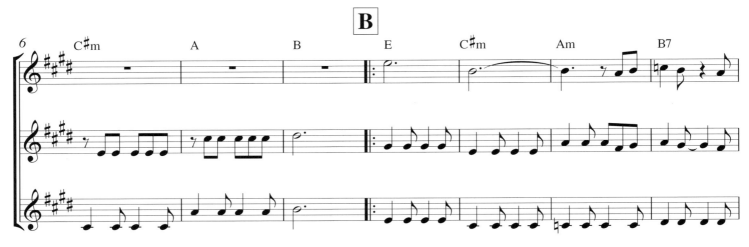

# Walk Don't Run

By Johnny Smith

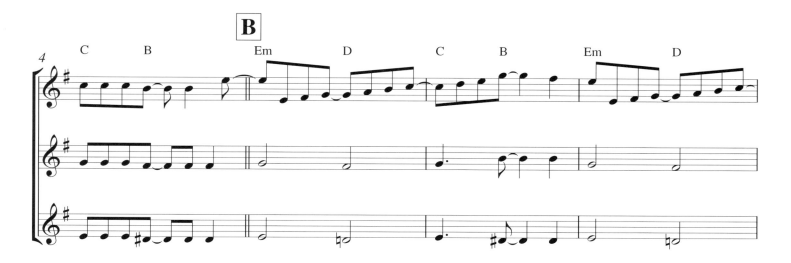

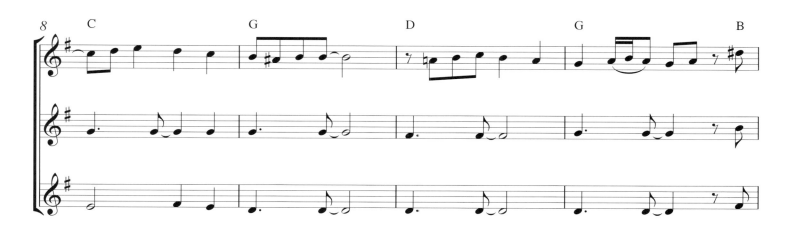

# Tequila

By Chuck Rio

# Wipe Out

By The Surfaris

Play drum solo by tapping on ukulele body.

## NOTES FROM THE ARRANGER

Arranging for three ukuleles can be challenging because of the instrument's limited range. In standard tuning (G-C-E-A), there is only one octave plus a major sixth between the open C string and fret 12 on the A string. Certain melodies easily span this distance and more, so compromises sometimes had to be made.

Not all ukuleles have the same number of frets. If your uke has fewer than 15 frets, you may need to play certain phrases an octave lower (especially in Part I). Some phrases have already been transposed up or down an octave—this was only done out of necessity and kept to a minimum. A few songs require every inch of available fretboard, but fret 15 on the first string (high C) is the limit, and this is extremely rare.

The three voices will sometimes cross as a result of range limitations. If Part III is considered to be the "bass" line, keep in mind that the lowest available "bass" notes are sometimes on the first string! However, if you own a baritone ukulele, almost all of the notes in Part III could be played an octave lower (except the open C string and C♯ on fret 1), thus providing a more effective bass line.

Despite the above caveats, I believe that the spirit of these songs has been preserved, and I hope you enjoy playing these arrangements as much as I enjoyed creating them. By the way, a fourth ensemble part can be added by strumming along with the chord symbols!

– Chad Johnson

## SOPRANO, CONCERT & TENOR FRETBOARD

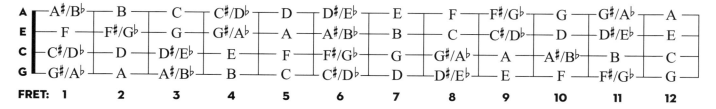

## BARITONE FRETBOARD

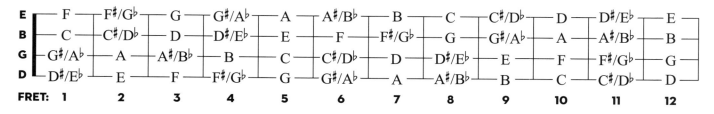